VIRGO

HOROSCOPE

& ASTROLOGY

2023

Mystic Cat

Suite 41906, 3/2237 Gold Coast HWY

Mermaid Beach, Queensland, 4218

Australia

Contents

VIRGO 2023
HOROSCOPE & ASTROLOGY

Four Weeks Per Month

Week 1 – Days 1 - 7

Week 2 – Days 8 - 14

Week 3 – Days 15 - 21

Week 4 – Days 22 – Month-end

VIRGO

Virgo Dates: August 23rd to September 22nd

Zodiac Symbol: Virgin

Element: Earth

Planet: Mercury

House: Sixth

Colors: Tan, warm yellow

Virgo

2023 AT A GLANCE

Eclipses

Hybrid Solar – April 20th

Penumbral Lunar – May 5th

Annular Solar – October 14th

Partial Lunar -October 28th

Equinoxes and Solstices

Spring - March 20th 21:25

Summer - June 21st 14:52

Fall – September 23rd 06:50

Winter – December 22nd 03:28

Mercury Retrogrades

December 29th Capricorn - January 18th Capricorn

April 21st Taurus – May 15th Taurus

August 23rd Virgo – September 15th Virgo

December 13th Capricorn - January 2[nd,] Sagittarius

2023 FULL MOONS

Wolf Moon: January 6th 23:09

Snow Moon: February 13th, 18:30

Worm Moon March 7th, 12:40

Pink Moon: April 6th, 04:37

Flower Moon: May 5th, 17:34

Strawberry Moon: June 4th, 03:42

Buck Moon: July 3rd, 11:40

Sturgeon Moon: August 1st, 18:32

Blue Moon: August 31st, 01:36

Corn, Harvest Moon: September 29th, 06:50

Hunters Moon: October 28th, 20:23

Beaver Moon: November 27th, 09:16

Cold Moon: December 27th, 00:34

2023 INGRESSES

When a planet moves into a new sign or house of the zodiac, it ingresses into the next area. This planetary movement creates an energy shift that can affect your life on many levels. It changes the tone, flavor, and energetic expression of life. Changing cosmic alignments can have detrimental or beneficial impacts on your life.

Some celestial bodies change every few days, others every few weeks, a few only have changes occurring every few years. The longer the time interval between a planet's ingress, the slower the effect on your life.

Cosmic vibrations ripple around your energy field and help raise your vibration, or conversely, lower your energy. It brings a time of change that can affect your life on many levels. Being aware of upcoming changes helps you research and stay mindful of how planetary ingresses may affect your world.

Faster Moving Ingresses

Mar 25, 2023, 11:46   Mars enters Cancer

May 20, 2023, 15:32   Mars enters Leo

Jul 10, 2023, 11:41   Mars enters Virgo

Aug 27, 2023, 13:20   Mars enters Libra

Oct 12, 2023, 04:04   Mars enters Scorpio

Nov 24, 2023, 10:15   Mars enters Sagittarius

Faster Moving Ingresses

Jan 3, 2023, 02:10	Venus enters Aquarius
Jan 27, 2023, 02:33	Venus enters Pisces
Feb 20, 2023, 07:56	Venus enters Aries
Mar 16, 2023, 22:34	Venus enters Taurus
Apr 11, 2023, 04:48	Venus enters Gemini
May 7, 2023, 14:25	Venus enters Cancer
Jun 5, 2023, 13:47	Venus enters Leo
Oct 9, 2023, 01:11	Venus enters Virgo
Nov 8, 2023, 09:31	Venus enters Libra
Dec 4, 2023, 18:51	Venus enters Scorpio
Dec 29, 2023, 20:24	Venus enters Sagittarius

Faster Moving Ingresses

Feb 11, 2023, 11:23	Mercury enters Aquarius
Mar 2, 2023, 22:52	Mercury enters Pisces
Mar 19, 2023, 04:24	Mercury enters Aries
Apr 3, 2023, 16:22	Mercury enters Taurus
Jun 11, 2023, 10:27	Mercury enters Gemini
Jun 27, 2023, 00:24	Mercury enters Cancer
Jul 11, 2023, 04:11	Mercury enters Leo
Jul 28, 2023, 21:32	Mercury enters Virgo
Oct 5, 2023, 00:09	Mercury enters Libra
Oct 22, 2023, 06:49	Mercury enters Scorpio
Nov 10, 2023, 06:25	Mercury enters Sagittarius
Dec 1, 2023, 14:32	Mercury enters Capricorn

Slower Moving Ingresses

Mar 7, 2023, 13:35	Saturn enters Pisces
Mar 23, 2023, 12:14	Pluto enters Aquarius
May 16, 2023, 17:21	Jupiter enters Taurus

THE MOON PHASES

New Moon (Dark Moon)

Waxing Crescent Moon

First Quarter Moon

Waxing Gibbous Moon

Full Moon

Waning Gibbous (Disseminating) Moon

Third (Last/Reconciling) Quarter Moon

Waning Crescent (Balsamic) Moon

2023

JANUARY
M	T	W	T	F	S	S
						1
2	3	4	5	6	7	8
9	10	11	12	13	14	15
16	17	18	19	20	21	22
23	24	25	26	27	28	29
30	31					

FEBRUARY
M	T	W	T	F	S	S
		1	2	3	4	5
6	7	8	9	10	11	12
13	14	15	16	17	18	19
20	21	22	23	24	25	26
27	28					

MARCH
M	T	W	T	F	S	S
		1	2	3	4	5
6	7	8	9	10	11	12
13	14	15	16	17	18	19
20	21	22	23	24	25	26
27	28	29	30	31		

APRIL
M	T	W	T	F	S	S
					1	2
3	4	5	6	7	8	9
10	11	12	13	14	15	16
17	18	19	20	21	22	23
24	25	26	27	28	29	30

MAY
M	T	W	T	F	S	S
1	2	3	4	5	6	7
8	9	10	11	12	13	14
15	16	17	18	19	20	21
22	23	24	25	26	27	28
29	30	31				

JUNE
M	T	W	T	F	S	S
			1	2	3	4
5	6	7	8	9	10	11
12	13	14	15	16	17	18
19	20	21	22	23	24	25
26	27	28	29	30		

JULY
M	T	W	T	F	S	S
					1	2
3	4	5	6	7	8	9
10	11	12	13	14	15	16
17	18	19	20	21	22	23
24	25	26	27	28	29	30
31						

AUGUST
M	T	W	T	F	S	S
1	2	3	4	5	6
7	8	9	10	11	12	13
14	15	16	17	18	19	20
21	22	23	24	25	26	27
28	29	30	31			

SEPTEMBER
M	T	W	T	F	S	S
				1	2	3
4	5	6	7	8	9	10
11	12	13	14	15	16	17
18	19	20	21	22	23	24
25	26	27	28	29	30	

OCTOBER
M	T	W	T	F	S	S
						1
2	3	4	5	6	7	8
9	10	11	12	13	14	15
16	17	18	19	20	21	22
23	24	25	26	27	28	29
30	31					

NOVEMBER
M	T	W	T	F	S	S
		1	2	3	4	5
6	7	8	9	10	11	12
13	14	15	16	17	18	19
20	21	22	23	24	25	26
27	28	29	30			

DECEMBER
M	T	W	T	F	S	S
				1	2	3
4	5	6	7	8	9	10
11	12	13	14	15	16	17
18	19	20	21	22	23	24
25	26	27	28	29	30	31

Time set to Coordinated Universal Time Zone

(UT±0)

Meteor Showers are on the date they peak.

JANUARY

Sun	Mon	Tue	Wed	Thu	Fri	Sat
1	2	3	4	5	6	7
8	9	10	11	12	13	14
15	16	17	18	19	20	21
22	23	24	25	26	27	28
29	30	31				

January 3rd - Quadrantids Meteor Shower. Jan 1st-5th

January 6th - Wolf Moon. Full Moon in Cancer 23:09

January 7th - Mercury at Inferior Conjunction

January 12th - Mars Retrograde ends in Gemini

January 15th - Last Quarter Moon in Libra 02:10

January 18th - Mercury Retrograde ends in Capricorn

January 21st - New Moon in Aquarius 20:55

January 22nd - Uranus Retrograde ends in Taurus January 22nd - Chinese New Year (Rabbit)

January 28th - First Quarter Moon in Taurus 15:19

January 30th - Mercury at Greatest Elong: 25.0°W

NEW MOON

FULL MOON

The Quadrantids Meteor Shower blazes across the night sky this week. A Full Moon in Cancer promotes healing quality that washes away outworn areas. After some soul-searching, you will find a lighter vibration around your life. It helps you invest your time and energy in developing regions that hold the most significant meaning in your life. Reshaping goals revolutionizes the potential in your world. You gain a glimpse of glittering possibility and soon thrive in a busy and dynamic environment. Harnessing the power of your creativity cracks the code to advancing life forward.

An important decision cracks the code to improving your life. You pour your energy into an area that draws pleasing results. It connects with a social aspect that nurtures companionship. You discover an authentic journey that brings well-being and happiness. It fosters a harmonious social life. It brings an end to delays as life moves forward, bringing an expansive and liberating phase that rekindles inspiration. It brings the motivation to expand the borders of your world.

A more rich life experience arrives to heal an aspect that has been out of alignment recently. It does help you release bottled-up emotions that have caused tension that limited your true potential. It underscores an atmosphere of acceptance that brings balance and lets you build new foundations. It generates a fresh start that promotes expansion in your personal life.

Mars retrograde ends in Gemini, and this sees an increase in drive, energy, and ambition. A business idea takes off and blossoms into growing your talents in a new area. Harnessing the magic within your creativity lets, you use the power of your skills to come up with viable options worth developing. You discover further leads that bring forward momentum into your life. It provides an avenue that advances your skills. It soon blossoms into a liberating chapter that cultivates change. It ushers in a dynamic and progressive time.

You get a leg up to a new area that offers an assignment that grows your skills. Assessing the potential helps give you the green light to move forward and advance your abilities into a dynamic environment. Being open to new opportunities facilitates change that opens life to an exciting flavor. You achieve a handsome reward by being open to new possibilities. It brings the news that lights a promising path towards growth.

Taking on a new area draws a pleasing result. It rekindles inspiration and gets you busy working on a passion project that uses your talents to improve life. The possibility to develop a joint project draws fruitful results. It brings an end to delays as you soon find heartening progress lights the path forward. Creativity blooms under sunny skies. Working on your craft brings fantastic results into your world.

Mercury retrograde ends in Capricorn. A New Moon in Aquarius at week's end. A lovely change enables you to nurture more personal aspects. It helps you create space to build a balanced and grounded energy around your home life. An area you seek to develop brings enriching and meaningful prospects into your life. You feel that life has more substance and significance as you concentrate on goals that hold the most significant meaning around your situation. Creating more balance and stability draws a pleasing result.

There will be important developments around your life soon; taking a closer look at the potential possible helps you unearth the right direction. You are ready for change, and a new chapter doesn't disappoint when it offers a trailblazing path forward. You hit your peak stride as you cultivate happiness and expansion in your social life.

Information arrives soon that offers a lighter chapter. It brings a chance to dream about the possibilities as you crack the code to a brighter chapter. You head towards an active time of engaging with your social life. It brings outings and opportunities that feel spontaneous and adventurous. Keeping life vivid and dynamic draws happy times that uplift the mood. You find the right flavor by adding a dash of variety to your life.

Chinese New Year of the Rabbit offers good luck and auspicious offerings for your life. The Rabbit symbolizes fertility, raising creativity and enabling you to grow a blossoming path forward for your life. A window of opportunity opens, and this helps you push stumbling blocks aside and rise to the occasion as you get busy and make the most of growing your life. It provides room to progress your talents into a new area. New possibilities tempt you towards an exciting landscape that is productive and innovative. Your willingness to explore various options helps you develop a winning trajectory.

Something extraordinary is about to appear in the road ahead for your life. It marks a time of happy surprises that bring a spontaneous element into your world. It ushers in a social aspect that feels enriching as it restores well-being and harmony to your spirit. Make yourself a priority; changes ahead beckon and tempt you towards expansion. It helps you break new ground.

Setting the bar higher brings a pleasing result. It helps you break past limitations and dive into an empowering phase of career growth. You build a bridge towards your vision by planning, preparing, and working towards your vision for future growth. Researching a unique area helps cultivate your talents and advance your skills. You stretch past your comfort zone and explore an exciting destination that calls your name.

FEBRUARY

Sun	Mon	Tue	Wed	Thu	Fri	Sat
			1	2	3	4
5	6	7	8	9	10	11
12	13	14	15	16	17	18
19	20	21	22	23	24	25
26	27	28				

February 1st - Imbolc

February 5th - Snow Moon. Full Moon in Leo 18:30

February 13th - Last Quarter Moon in Scorpio 16:01

February 16th - Saturn in Conjunction with Sun

February 20th - New Moon in Pisces 07:08

February 27th - First Quarter Moon in Gemini 08:06

NEW MOON

FULL MOON

A Full Moon in Leo lets life blossom; it gives you intuition and wisdom. You benefit from taking a little worn path that has you exploring a side journey that is right for your soul. It is a boost to your spirit, it has you focusing on improving your immediate environment, and it brings results you can appreciate. Life picks up the pace, which takes you to a more socially active chapter that offers a wellspring of potential. It provides a gateway towards a fresh chapter that creates space to heal the past and nurture your current environment. It culminates in a journey that triggers a path forward. It lets you invest your time in a meaningful area that offers personal growth. It is a soothing salve for your soul. Nurturing stable foundations promotes well-being and harmony in your life.

You are ready to remove areas that no longer serve your higher good. Sweeping away outworn layers does reshuffle the deck of fate. It brings a valuable path to nurture your home environment as you discover abilities that tempt you towards growth. You enter a phase of expansion and begin developing your journey towards a new level of being. Change and evolution are a continual cycle in your world. It brings a time that sees you being more expressive about what you seek and need in your life. You create space to chase your vision. Some lovely changes are ready to flow into your world. It signifies a time that draws an abundant environment. It brings more stability to your personal life.

The planet Mercury slips into your sixth house of health, well-being, wellness, and vitality. It brings an emphasis on self-development and making yourself a priority. Nurturing areas that feel sublime and draw balance into your surroundings hits a sweet note in your life this week. It is a curious time that offers a remarkable chance to develop your personal life. It brings intimate conversations that resonate with feelings of romance. It does have you dreaming about the possibilities. Developing a heart bond becomes a strong focus, it takes a little while to come together, but the rewards are worth it.

Luck flows into your life when news arrives that bestows blessings. This good fortune does fund a new pathway towards growth. It places you in the box seat to develop your vision, and it does bring a project that is a positive sign that things are on track as progression looms overhead. There is an emphasis on creativity that dials up the potential possible.

There is a lot of emphasis on home and family at this time. It does bring hope, and it offers a direct link towards an enterprising time. It rules creativity, and you can tackle projects that have been on the back burner for some time, which advances life. The opportunity to finish endeavors is running high. It does see life becoming more accessible and more abundant.

Saturn in conjunction with the Sun. New Moon in Pisces. A meticulous approach to improving your circumstances brings opportunities that create a bridge to a brighter chapter. It emphasizes self-expression, identity, and creativity. It brings an efficient and productive time that brings you closer to your goals. Growing your skills and refining your talents has a powerful effect on improving the foundations in your life. It sparks a path that advances towards an engaging time.

Changes arrive that create a growth-orientated phase. It brings new demands to your life. And while these responsibilities can feel demanding at times, it gets a chance to grow your skills, and you soon develop a cohesive plan that builds a stable foundation. The fires of your inspiration open a path towards advancing your circumstances. Your life is moving forward towards a new assignment. This project makes a big difference in your life as it enables you to have more time to focus on your passions. It brings opportunities to improve your situation, which culminates in a time of expansion. A sunny aspect arrives in your world.

You can advance the potential possible in your life by staying open to new pathways of growth and learning. It does emphasize a time of increasing creativity that enables you to spot areas of significant potential. You shine a light on expanding your skillset and soon become busy with new assignments.

You have the time and motivation to focus on advancing goals. It sets the essence of manifestation in motion that gently shifts your focus towards a long-term destination. Creative energy brews up a storm of potential that ushers in change. Metamorphosis is occurring that cracks the code to a new path. It draws renewal, rejuvenation, and healing. It elevates potential and kicks the cobwebs to the curb.

You are in the process of creating change. It helps you move forward towards developing a cherished dream. It does bring a chance to network and get involved with your social life. You scoop the pool and discover a journey that ushers in new potential. It brings a clear path that lets you dive in and embrace advancing your world.

News arrives that gets a boost; this information offers a nugget of gold for your personal life. An area you nurture takes on a life of its own and brings an active growth and expansion phase. It is a time of rapid growth that teaches you the value of resilience. You navigate a complex environment and come out a winner. It lets you set sail on a timely voyage of improving your circumstances. A gateway ahead brings a journey of excitement and adventure. It is a time of waiting for new information. It lets you touch down in a more abundant landscape. News arrives to get the ball rolling forward.

MARCH

Sun	Mon	Tue	Wed	Thu	Fri	Sat
			1	2	3	4
5	6	7	8	9	10	11
12	13	14	15	16	17	18
19	20	21	22	23	24	25
26	27	28	29	30	31	

March 7th - Worm Moon. Full Moon in Virgo 12:40

March 15th - Last Quarter Moon: Sagittarius 02:08
March 15th - Neptune in Conjunction with Sun

March 17th - Mercury at Superior Conjunction

March 20th - Ostara/Spring Equinox 21:25

March 21st - New Moon in Pisces 17:22

March 29th - First Quarter Moon in Cancer 02:32

NEW MOON

FULL MOON

A Full Moon in Virgo brings a catalyst for change; it has you taking a leap of faith on a journey forward. You discover areas that are therapeutic for your spirit. This self-development heals old wounds that may be holding you back from achieving your best. It does involve a time of nurturing the magic within. Take time to draw more stability into your life by slowing down and focusing on one step at a time. Once you ground your energy, a remarkable shift takes you towards a happy chapter. You experience a moment of healing, and clarity soon comes calling to bring insight into your deepest goals.

The work you do on your inner terrain is invaluable. As the pieces fall into place and as you heal the missing fragments of your soul, you become whole. This journey of self-development is likely to bring a breakthrough moment, a reawakening to all that you can achieve. Change is surrounding you; taking time to resolve limitations does create space to usher in new potential.

You shed light on something revealing. As this confidential information reveals, you see the right decision to make. It does bring clarity and motivates you to create the changes necessary to open the doors wide on a new chapter. As with all life lessons, you learn and grow during this insightful time. Your creativity is rising; this draws innovative solutions and does manifest the path towards a new area.

Saturn glides into Pisces, and this emphasizes your seventh house of partnerships, business matters, diplomacy, and agreements. Saturn is a planet that promotes structure and order in your life. It teaches that patience, discipline, and tradition offer advancement and growth. Developing stable foundations brings a solid basis for expanding your life when the time feels right to embark on growing your life. Discipline, and hard work, will bring advancement to your door. You have plenty of energy at your disposal to focus on your goals. It lets you achieve headway on developing a venture that holds plenty of promise. It could lead to an entrepreneurial direction or a business path that captures your interest.

Focusing on strategy helps you leap forward. You enter a highly productive chapter that is ripe for expansion. A cluster of activity is looming; it creates hotspots of potential that you can mine to come up with hidden gems. You enter a phase of growth, expansion, and heightened potential. It welcomes a surge of new possibilities as tempting options flood your environment. It unleashes your creativity in an area worth your time and effort. Drafting your goals lets, you have a plan to make sure that things reach fruition. It gives the push needed to take your abilities to a new level. Scaling back on the demands on your time, draw dividends.

The Spring Equinox this week puts the spring in your step. Life heads to an upswing that offers solid growth and progression. It brings an extended time that paves the way forward to a more stable and balanced time of expanding your life outwardly. It brings a life-affirming area into focus. It lets you make headway is towards advancing your life. Breaking free of constraints and let you dive into a refreshing aspect that helps ignite unique potential.

An emphasis on improving your life opens a new page of potential. It is an enriching time that offers a sense of support and connection. It lets you step out with friends and colleagues. It brings a fruitful time of lively discussions and thoughtful dialogues. It connects you with unique people and characters who light up refreshing possibilities across the board of your social life. Combining this support with increasing stability anchors your energy in a grounded foundation.

A magical time ahead brings improvement into your life. Under this influence, you reach for harmony and connection in your world. It brings a fantastic time that nurtures abundance. It connects you with room to grow your social life. Taking time to reflect on the past is instrumental as it helps release outworn areas that limit progress. It yields the type of stability that refuels energy tanks and rejuvenates your life from the ground up. Expanding your circle of friends nourishes well-being and draws robust equilibrium to your foundations.

Mars lands in your eleventh house of blessings, belonging, associations, and networking. Mars seeks to raise your confidence with energy that is assertive. Being proactive and taking action enables growth to occur. You move forward with courage and daring towards desires. Feeling energized and ambitious, you scope out areas that offer rising prospects for your life. An upgrade is coming for your situation. A burst of new energy flows into your life and gives your goals wings. Strategy, planning, and focus help you create the changes you seek. It gives you a better grasp of achieving your vision. Life picks up momentum, and you begin to thrive in this active and dynamic environment. You find an outlet for your excess energy; it is a busy and happy time.

A breath of fresh air enters your life that sparks a sense of reinvention. It does spotlight a path of expansion, growth, and adventure. A leap of faith brings new people into your life. As you explore the possibilities, you get a sense of wanting to move out of your comfort zone and achieve a significant result. It is a time that grows your confidence, bringing new pathways to explore. A surge of positive and inspirational energy supports expansion. It emphasizes growth and progressing practical matters. It unlocks a gateway to a brighter future that offers many blessings for your life. Mapping out ideas brings new and innovative options to light. It kicks off a daring journey that lifts the lid on achieving gold in your life.

Sun	Mon	Tue	Wed	Thu	Fri	Sat
						1
2	3	4	5	6	7	8
9	10	11	12	13	14	15
16	17	18	19	20	21	22
23	24	25	26	27	28	29
30						

April 6th - Pink Moon. Full Moon in Libra 04:37

April 11th - Jupiter in Conjunction with Sun
April 11th - Mercury at Greatest Elong: 19.5°E

April 13th - Last Quarter Moon in Capricorn 09:11

April 20th - New Moon in Taurus 04:12
April 20th - Hybrid Solar Eclipse

April 21st - Mercury Retrograde begins in Taurus

April 22nd - Lyrids Meteor Shower. April 16-25

April 27th - First Quarter Moon in Leo 21:20

NEW MOON

FULL MOON

The Full Moon in Libra promotes balanced foundations. It's time to mend the scars of the past. Dealing with areas that linger on your awareness does create space for healing. Under this influence, you transform your potential, which is instrumental in letting something new into your world. As you dismantle any blocks that hold you back, you become ready to embrace a new chapter. It does lead to change that ignites your imagination. You enter a self-expressive phase that harnesses the power of your creativity to create steady evolution. An area you discover becomes a priority; this gives you a clean slate of potential. It brings an exciting phase that inspires your mind. It marks a time when you can chase your dreams and relish the possible results.

A turning point brings in sweeping changes. It does slow your situation down to some extent, yet this can be seen as welcome; it gives you a chance to integrate these changes into your life. Focusing on emotional wellness, you process unresolved sensitivities—a vacation through the past heals and creates an environment that nurtures your soul.

An option is arriving that bodes well for your life. It does draw answers to long-held questions. As you shift towards a new change of pace, you discover a direction that connects you to your dreams. It is a transition that reinvents and rejuvenates. A completely new perspective is possible; it brings a fresh start that lets you gain valuable traction on your vision.

Jupiter sees the path ahead in conjunction with the Sun, glittering with possibilities. A little worn avenue opens and brings luck into your world. It offers a journey that grows your abilities and refines your talents. News on the horizon brings insight into developing a path that captures the essence of manifestation. It expands your life outwardly towards new goals when you discover a refreshing destination comes calling. It lets you get involved with an area that bodes well for your life.

Contemplating the path ahead and future life direction draws a valid result. It offers a chance to branch out and develop an area intrinsic to home life. Look for heightened security around the home base. It brings an opportunity to mingle with friends that draw rejuvenation and well-being into your life.

The conditions are ripe to extend your reach and embrace a journey that faces forward. It lets you swim upstream to new possibilities, and you soon discover smoother waters that glide you into a particular time of self-development. You draw profitable opportunities that improve circumstances. Life-affirming endeavors capture the essence of creativity as they bring innovative options to light. It brings balance and stability into your home life. It paves the way to a chapter that offers liveliness. It lets you turn a corner and embrace a time of happiness and gain.

A New Moon in Taurus at the week's end facilitates change. You find that creative opportunities spark your curiosity and interest. Remembering your dreams and getting in touch with your intuition guide you towards new adventures in your social life. All things to do with creativity, intuition, and emotions encourage growth in your world. New possibilities soon flow into your life. This tremendous energy attracts an inspiring outlook that cultivates change by listening to your most authentic self.

Being involved with growing your life brings growth to your circle of friends. News arrives that points you towards a path of rising opportunities that involve developing friendships. It opens the door to the possibility of a new relationship for your love life. You discover that anything is possible when you listen to your instincts. You receive serendipitous signs that help point you towards a more prosperous and fulfilling life experience. You sense that something big is around the corner as you work on improving your circumstances. A lighter energy flow brings strength and creative power that cultivates inspiring ideas. Prioritizing your goals adds a potent and robust aspect to the mix of manifestation in your life. Setting aspirations enables planning that helps grow your life in a unique direction. You see a deeply held desire reach fruition by meticulously working towards your vision.

Lyrids Meteor Shower illuminates bright possibilities ahead for interpersonal bonds in your life. It brings good luck to your social life. It does get a perk that is a boost to your spirit. You discover the answer is within reach. It brings a journey that offers room to improve your world. You let down your guard and focus on developing a situation that captures your attention. Your social life is humming along; invitations, communication, and news ahead keep you busy.

A social environment links you up with kindred spirits. It does bring a chance to develop your social circle. It ignites remarkably refreshing inspiration. It does light up pathways towards growth. There are impressive gains to be achieved on the social scene. It brings an enormously significant chapter that offers new friendships. Things are on the move; it begins a positive trend that takes your goals to the next level. It brings the gift of harmony into your social life. The conditions are perfect for progression. You head out and take an active role in improving your circumstances.

An invitation ahead offers a diversion that has you mingling with companions who support and nurture your life. You can embrace a more social chapter; this draws abundance and lifts your spirit higher. New goals and options tempt you forward. Making the most of this potential opens your world to companions who offer advancement.

MAY

Sun	Mon	Tue	Wed	Thu	Fri	Sat
	1	2	3	4	5	6
7	8	9	10	11	12	13
14	15	16	17	18	19	20
21	22	23	24	25	26	27
28	29	30	31			

52

May 1ˢᵗ - Mercury at Inferior Conjunction
May 1ˢᵗ Pluto retrograde begins in Aquarius

May 5ᵗʰ - Flower Moon. Full Moon in Scorpio 17:34
May 5ᵗʰ - Penumbral Lunar Eclipse

May 6ᵗʰ - Eta Aquarids Meteor Shower, April 19ᵗʰ - May 28ᵗʰ

May 9ᵗʰ - Uranus in Conjunction with Sun

May 12ᵗʰ - Last Quarter Moon in Aquarius 14:28

May 15ᵗʰ - Mercury Retrograde ends in Taurus

May 19ᵗʰ - New Moon in Taurus 15:54

May 27ᵗʰ - First Quarter Moon in Virgo 15:22

May 29ᵗʰ - Mercury at Greatest Elong: 24.9°W

NEW MOON

FULL MOON

Pluto's planet goes retrograde this week before a full Moon in Scorpio combines with a penumbral lunar eclipse. Significant change opens ahead that wipes the slate clean. It creates space to draw in new energy that sweetens and grows the situation. News is coming that guides the path forward. It helps overcome blocks, which is instrumental in healing and nurturing the case. It brings clarity as a puzzle piece reveals; you discover the path forward clears. It creates a stable platform from which to grow better bonds. It helps you turn a corner and enjoy smooth sailing.

Your intuition guides you correctly; open communication and transparency are crucial to nurturing interpersonal bonds. Summoning tremendous courage, you face the future with a brave heart. The tides turn in your favor, and you land in an enriching environment that draws well-being and harmony into your life. Focusing on sharing from your heart draws stability. It is instrumental in creating space for a new chapter of potential to emerge.

Forgiveness swirls around your life and tempts you towards improving social bonds. It anchors your energy in improving the potential possible. Significant changes overhead connect you with new possibilities that will enhance your world. It brings a social aspect that draws a refreshing change. It connects you to expanding horizons that usher in a chance of healing and re-establishing solid foundations.

In conjunction with the Sun, Uranus promotes surprise information, spontaneous occurrences, and unexpected happenings. Changes ahead help you settle into a new groove, a new way of living your life. It brings plot twists in the form of happy surprises that connect to improvement around your social life. It fuels inspiration and conveys the motivation to develop your social life proactively. It connects you with kindred spirits who understand your take on life. It draws an auspicious time of relaxing conversations, and this brings a focus on well-being and happiness. You direct attention towards spending more time in a supportive and nurturing environment. Events online up to nourish your soul as the borders of your world expand.

An opportunity will arrive for you soon. It opens a gateway towards a fresh start. It brings social opportunities that add richness to your life. Broadening the scope of your world is a catalyst for growth as it opens new pathways that see you expanding life outwardly. It illustrates a time of lively discussions as invitations to mingle flow into your life. The path ahead clears, bringing an open road of potential. It triggers a freedom-loving chapter of adventures that gets the ball rolling on expanding the horizons in your life. A sweet surprise ahead begins a positive trend that positively influences your life as it marks a new beginning that creates space to nurture your dreams.

Mercury retrograde ends in Taurus, bringing a lighter vibration into your social life. Trusting your instincts helps you find balance as you let go of doubt and indecision. Removing the fear of limitations nurtures an open road of potential. A new option emerges that lets you dive into the deep end and live life to the fullest. It brings a social aspect that quenches your thirst for connection and companionship. You release the shackles of past issues and live your truth as you forge a unique path forward for your life.

A better balance in your home/work life ahead lets you create more space to nurture meaningful areas in your life. Clearing away limitations and expanding your horizons brings a high note to your social life. It lights a positive path that offers fresh inspiration. Improving your circumstances are creates a breakthrough that takes you towards a happy chapter.

Past struggles fade away as a healing influence sweeps away outworn energy. You head towards a time that favors growth; a crossroads ahead brings a decision that helps you cut troublesome aspects. It brings improvement that sets the tone for developing stable foundations that enrich your world. Exploring leads brings change and progression that marks a turning point.

It is a great time that gets your goals and dreams on the front burner. A new role crops up, bringing a project that lets you channel your energy productively. It heightens security and enables you to make notable tracks on improving the foundations in your life. A new cycle is coming that takes your aspirations further, and this hits the right note in your life. Positive news on the horizon shines a light on a working opportunity.

Developing your abilities and nurturing your talents brings change and advancement into view. You decide that cracks the code to the path ahead as it gets more excellent stability and security into your world. It transpires into a journey that offers room to advance your gifts into a new area. Working with your skills initiates an enterprising chapter that involves higher learning.

Positive news arrives soon. Heightened opportunities ahead lead to a progressive phase of social engagement. It brings extra support and a sense of connection to your door. It lets you chart a course towards an enriching chapter that ushers in laughter, music, and lively discussions. It brings thoughtful dialogue and helpful advice to the forefront of your world; in this fertile ground, creativity blossoms.

JUNE

Sun	Mon	Tue	Wed	Thu	Fri	Sat
				1	2	3
4	5	6	7	8	9	10
11	12	13	14	15	16	17
18	19	20	21	22	23	24
25	26	27	28	29	30	

ASTROLOGY

June 4th - Strawberry Full Moon: Sagittarius 03:42

June 4th - Venus at Greatest Elong: 45.4°E

June 10th - Last Quarter Moon in Pisces 19:31

June 17th - Saturn Retrograde begins in Pisces

June 18th - New Moon in Cancer 04:38

June 21st - Midsummer/Litha Solstice 14:52

June 26th - First Quarter Moon in Libra 07:50

June 30th - Neptune Retrograde begins in Pisces

NEW MOON

FULL MOON

Venus reaches the greatest elongation as a full Moon in Sagittarius blooms. Beautiful symmetry is coming, drawing healing and closure into your world. It brings the energy that is quite therapeutic for your mood as it offers lightness and harmony. It forms the basis of grounded energy to expand your life. Consequently, you head towards an uptick of potential that offers new leads ripe for development. Shedding outworn areas resolves the issues that have limited progress. It cracks the code to a brighter chapter ahead.

You can honor your wild and rebellious tendencies and embrace the path that comes calling. Heeding the yearning within your heart stokes the fires of inspiration. It is a journey that unearths hidden gems of possibility. Sifting and sorting through the various options help you come up with a winner. It lets you create clear goals that mark the right way forward. Taking down barriers harnesses the sense of manifestation that offers new territory and an expansive view to contemplate.

A highly creative and self-expressive phase is looming. You set sail on a voyage that offers happiness and self-development. Listening to your emotions taps into the correct path. It lets you show your talents to a broader audience and has you exploring new pathways of growth and prosperity. Fortune shines upon your life as you transition towards a positive chapter that expands your horizons into new areas.

Mercury moves to your tenth house of enterprise, ambitions, and career achievements. It brings the news into your working life that sparks promotion, advancement, and recognition. It enables you to navigate a path ahead that delivers a stable environment to grow your career. A doorway opens, and a new role on offer draws an enticing glimpse of future possibilities. It places the spotlight on increasing your abilities and nurturing your talents.

The future is ready to bless your life with new potential. Something comes which bolsters your mood and inspires growth. You are developing new dreams as it starts a cycle of expansion and evolution. Enthusiasm and creativity skyrocket, bringing new possibilities into your life. The sky is the limit; a personal project you work on soon takes on a life of its own.

Greener pastures beckon, and new information ahead helps you turn a corner and head towards growth. Information arrives swiftly to inspire change. It lets you move towards expansion as it opens a journey of abundance and prosperity. The wheels are in motion, and soon new options appear to inspire change. It lets you touch down on a promising path that facilitates the development of new projects and endeavors.

At the week's end, the New Moon in Cancer before Midsummer/Litha Solstice reveals a positive snapshot of potential ahead that lifts the lid on growing your world. It draws movement around your larger goals which help you create inroads towards advancing your plans. It paves the way forward for a dynamic time of learning a new area. It brings productive and busy energy into your working life. You knuckle down and get busy with the task at hand. As you make traction on improving your bottom line, you enjoy a lighter flow of energy that adds robust foundations to your life. It lets you gain traction on improving your world. You hit the jackpot when a windfall option makes itself known. It enables you to negotiate the path ahead and discover golden nuggets of potential. Unearthing new leads gives you a clue of new possibilities that flow into your world to tempt you forward. It has you in sync with expanding your life, which grows your life in a new direction. You carve out time for yourself and embrace rising prosperity.

This week reveals an ideal time that ushers in new possibilities for your social life. It supplies plenty of inspirational ideas to contemplate. Options to mingle keep you on your toes. It triggers impromptu get-togethers with friends, and this supports harmony and well-being. The path forward lights an engaging time of sharing with those who support your world. It brings golden opportunities that point the way forward.

Neptune goes retrograde in Pisces, which helps dispel illusions. It helps you base plans on areas that offer tangible results and realistic outcomes. Information arrives that enables you to get busy manifesting your dreams. An area comes calling that allows you to build growth and progress in your life. You discover an original path that feels like the right fit for your abilities. It brings an important project that links you to a social aspect that adds an exciting flavor to your life.

It begins a new phase in your life that helps you plot a course towards advancing your working life. Consistency and balance draw grounded foundations that let you move sustainably towards your vision for future growth. It brings a highly productive chapter that enables you to work with your abilities and refine your talents. You create inroads towards advancing life forward.

You are the captain of your ship; growing your world sparks a journey that leaves you feeling optimistic about rising prospects in your life. You land a prime role that brings new responsibilities and options that inspire growth. Working with your abilities and refining your skills helps you extend your reach into new areas worth your time. It lets you break free from restrictive patterns as new possibilities light a path onward. It brings a focus on developing a career path that highlights improving your bottom line. It brings rocket fuel for inspiration and creativity ahead.

JULY

Sun	Mon	Tue	Wed	Thu	Fri	Sat
						1
2	3	4	5	6	7	8
9	10	11	12	13	14	15
16	17	18	19	20	21	22
23	24	25	26	27	28	29
30	31					

July 1st - Mercury at Superior Conjunction

July 3rd - Buck Moon. Full Moon in Capricorn. Supermoon 11:40

July 10th - Last Quarter Moon in Aries 01:48

July 17th - New Moon in Cancer 18:32

July 23rd - Venus retrograde begins in Leo

July 25th - First Quarter Moon in Libra 22:06

July 28th - Delta Aquarids Meteor Shower. July 12th - August 23rd

NEW MOON

FULL MOON

The Mercury at Superior conjunction. Full Moon in Capricorn, Supermoon. The past has been a time of learning and growth that held you in good stead. Currently, a big reveal brings insight into a situation that may have been troubling you. Once you gain clarity into this area, it helps you draw healing into your surroundings. It lets you remove the outworn layers and get involved in moving your life forward towards a journey of happiness. New options beckon and take you on a path of discovery. A refreshing change is coming that opens an avenue of growth. It lets you get life on track as new possibilities are on offer soon.

You enter into a transition that may feel jarring at first. It is the significant shift forward you have been seeking. It brings new friends and companions into your life, which offers a refreshing social aspect.

Opportunities to spread your wings empower you to reach for your dreams. It brings a change to your home life that has you rebuilding your situation from the ground up. Getting back to basics builds a stable foundation that draws balance and harmony into your world. You enter a refreshing time that marks healing and release. It lets you close the door on past issues and stay in sync with your vision for future growth. Releasing the outworn energy in your life helps you turn the corner and head towards greener pastures in your life. The Full Moon washes away areas that seek release during this therapeutic time.

The planet Mercury makes itself known in your twelfth house of closure and endings. Retreating from everyday activities creates a refuge where you can tune into your intuition and reveal insight and clarity about the path ahead. An emphasis on improving your foundations sees circumstances shift and change as you utilize past lessons to create a bridge towards a happier time. It heralds an end of difficulties that allows you to achieve closure on a difficult phase and turn the page on a fresh chapter.

As you dig deeper into your future goals and aspirations, you discover insight into the path ahead. Perhaps some areas need shelving, while others are ripe for the picking. Clearing the way forward takes you towards an extended time of transformation. It brings sweeping changes that offer evolution and progress. It sets the stage for a creative chapter that provides a stable basis for growing your world.

A theme of closure and release draws healing. Indeed, changes ahead set life ablaze with new options. It lets you pivot away from problems and embrace a newfound sense of belonging. Unlocking the key to your creativity sees your ideas spreading like wildfire. It helps you unleash your abilities into an exciting area that tips the scales in your favor. It puts you in contact with like-minded people who bring a sense of community and harmony into your world, which is refreshing.

This week a New Moon in Cancer brings a favorable planetary aspect for researching and planning the path forward. Reaching for your dreams brings new options. It does open a clear way that brings growth and opportunity. Setting aspirations is the first step in noticing the signs that tempt you forward. There is such a rich and diverse landscape to explore; your imagination and intuition guide the way ahead. As you discover a fabulous route towards your vision, a sense of adventure awakens. Exciting news draws you out in a community setting.

You transition forwards towards a wonderfully abundant chapter. It draws bustling activity and offers enterprising options to explore. It has you thinking strategically about the future; you launch towards a phase that lets you put your plans in place. Mapping out your goals creates the stepping stones towards achieving your vision. It is an enriching chapter that brings a fresh start to your life.

A lovely perk arrives in your life, and it does see the path ahead glimmering with new information. This news encourages a shift forward; it has you exploring an area that makes your heart sing. It moves your potential up a notch and brings a trailblazing journey towards developing your life. Going after your dreams does draw luck and good fortune; it brings a significant change resulting from the expansion you are currently undergoing.

Venus retrograde begins in Leo, which impedes progressing your romantic life. Slowing down may help; it draws balance and lets you plot a course towards a grounded chapter. You will receive new information soon that brings good news. While it does drive essential changes, it enables you to navigate the path ahead and delivers a more stable environment. It does see you making headway on a goal that is dear to your heart. The past is giving you a great deal of insight. It does bring motivation to continue to evolve and grow your life.

Venus in retrograde offers an outstanding opportunity to dive into self-development and learn to express your inherent sense of creativity. The conditions are superb to dig deep and reveal greater insight and clarity around future goals. It does bring a slower pace that lets you integrate change and journey towards abundance.

An opportunity will come a-knocking soon. The planet Venus has put the brakes on developing your romantic life, but you can create space for a fresh chapter to emerge. Initiating new projects sets plans into motion that unfold into a path that inspires and delights. You can manifest your happiness and progress in your abilities. A doorway appears and tempts you forward. It brings a valuable turning point you can embrace.

AUGUST

Sun	Mon	Tue	Wed	Thu	Fri	Sat
		1	2	3	4	5
6	7	8	9	10	11	12
13	14	15	16	17	18	19
20	21	22	23	24	25	26
27	28	29	30	31		

August 1ˢᵗ - Full Sturgeon Moon in Aquarius Supermoon 18:32

August 8ᵗʰ - Last Quarter Moon in Taurus 10:28

August 10ᵗʰ - Mercury at Greatest Elong: 27.4°E

August 12ᵗʰ - Perseids Meteor Shower July 17ᵗʰ - Aug 24ᵗʰ

August 16ᵗʰ - New Moon in Leo 09:37

August 23ʳᵈ - Mercury Retrograde begins in Virgo

August 24ᵗʰ - First Quarter Moon in Sagittarius 09:57

August 27ᵗʰ - Saturn at Opposition

August 29ᵗʰ - Uranus Retrograde begins in Taurus

August 31ˢᵗ - Full Moon, Supermoon, Blue Moon in Pisces 01:36

NEW MOON

FULL MOON

Full Moon, Supermoon in Aquarius promotes insight and clarity. You enter a time that brings understanding into your life, nurturing grounded energy that draws healing. Your top priorities are peace, serenity, and stability. Focusing on the basics illustrates a new flow of energy into your environment. It lets things settle down as you pick up the pieces and begin to progress forward. It brings a spiritual journey into focus that helps rejuvenate your energy and release the pain.

Your mood becomes brighter and lighter as harmony shifts into focus. Concerns fall away, bringing positive change to your environment. Your pioneering spirit harnesses the power of resilience; this lets you turn a corner and head towards new potential. News arrives that switches you onto a new area. You notice the rhythm and pace of life pick up, drawing a welcome result. It brings a time that lets you reap the rewards of expansion.

Some changes ahead can feel disconcerting. It brings a time of removing outworn layers and healing the past. It takes you towards transformation. A change of priorities has you thinking about the future in a new light. You reach a fork in the road that sees you veer towards a new direction. It heightens confidence and draws a refreshing chapter of expanding your life. Wiping the slate clean illustrates new possibilities that soothe your spirit and refresh your inspiration. It brings a warm time that enriches your life and blesses your world.

Perseids meteor shower lights an exciting path forward this week. New foundations emerge in your life that wipes the slate clean. Being proactive about seeking out opportunities draws a pleasing result for your life. It connects you with an upbeat time that sees life moving faster. Meeting new people brings a fresh start that offers a rosy time for developing interpersonal bonds. Making yourself a priority puts your needs and desires front and center. It allows you to expand your life and connect with a companion who nurtures a wellspring of potential in your social life. It has you exploring a journey that feels right for your soul.

Indeed, the plot thickens as you reveal new information that gives you fresh insight into the path ahead. Fun and friendship bring light and laughter to your social life. Change surrounds your energy; it is a time earmarked for new possibilities. Dissolving stagnant patterns removes the blocks and opens the gateway forward.

Life heats up with new potential as you reveal a unique path forward. The seeds planted blossom into a way of meaning and substance. It indicates that new growth is ready to blossom in your life. New options ahead bring the gift of choice. An enterprising time lets you make tracks towards nurturing your abilities. It draws a new project and an exciting phase of expansion. It brings a change of direction that inspires growth.

The New Moon in Leo fosters a significant change. It brings a chapter that empowers and enriches your life. Being proactive draws a pleasing result as swift improvements follow the expansion of horizons around your life. You ramp up the potential possible by being flexible and adaptive to change. Communication arrives that shines the light around deepening friendships. An opportunity for collaboration offers growth and a sense of kinship. Your perseverance and resilience draw dividends. It places you in the proper alignment to improve your situation. Fortune and luck are arriving soon to draw blessings into your world.

There is a strong emphasis on improving your life that lights the way forward. This adjustment helps you move away from draining areas that have left you feeling depleted. A focus on creative planning lets you develop innovative ideas that resonate strongly. It is a time of good fortune that provides a path that glitters with possibilities. It does have you feeling optimistic about the future.

You shift direction in the chapter ahead. It does see changes flowing that are sustainable as well as advantageous. Focusing on progressing this path draws a dividend. It lets you move forward in a structured manner. It brings a phase that is thoughtful and purposeful. Setting your intentions kicks off a dynamic phase of progressing an exciting goal.

Uranus retrograde begins in Taurus. Full Moon, Supermoon, Blue Moon in Pisces on the last day of the month. Your perseverance draws dividends as you approach a turning point that gives you an exciting sign that things are changing for the better. It heralds an end of difficulties, allowing you to achieve closure on a difficult phase that tested you on many levels. Opportunity comes knocking as you expand your life. New possibilities flow into your world and create a soothing balm that resolves outworn energy.

Being actively involved in exploring options lets you take a proactive stance that draws a pleasing result. It washes away outworn energy and creates space to nurture the interpersonal ties that hold meaning in your life. It lifts flagging energy and offers a more social environment. Spending time with a valued friend brings the type of rejuvenation that is rocket fuel for your imagination.

You can shut the door on a painful chapter and achieve closure. Expect improvement in personal and social areas. It does let you embrace developing your life, and as you nurture connections, it breathes fresh air into your environment. Constructive dialogue with friends brings new ideas and possibilities. It captures the essence of rejuvenation that gets you ready to start afresh. It brings harmony flowing into your world and gives you the right foundations that draw stability. You usher in a social aspect that brings blessings into your world.

Sun	Mon	Tue	Wed	Thu	Fri	Sat
					1	2
3	4	5	6	7	8	9
10	11	12	13	14	15	16
17	18	19	20	21	22	23
24	25	26	27	28	29	30

September 4th - Venus Retrograde ends in Leo
September 4th - Jupiter Retrograde begins Taurus

September 6th - Last Quarter Moon in Gemini 22:21
September 6th - Mercury at Inferior Conjunction

September 15th - New Moon in Virgo 01:40
September 15th - Mercury Retrograde ends in Virgo

September 19th - Neptune at Opposition

September 22nd - Mercury at Greatest Elong 17.9°W
September 22nd - First Quarter Moon Sagittarius 19:32

September 23rd - Mabon/Fall Equinox. 06:50

September 29th - Corn Moon. Harvest Full Moon. Supermoon in Aries 09:58

NEW MOON

FULL MOON

Venus retrograde ends in Leo. Jupiter retrograde begins in Taurus this week. Expect improvement in your personal and social life as a more abundant flow of energy supports developing relationship bonds when Venus is in a direct phase. New possibilities spark a journey you can feel pleased about progressing. It involves the social chapter that is enchanting; the magic of mingling does wonders for your sense of well-being. You cultivate a positive outlook and nurture a social scene that activates invitations and possibilities to network. Engaging conversations with fascinating companions hit a sweet spot in your life.

A happy chapter is coming that ushers in the new energy. It brings a journey that inspires and rejuvenates your vision. Fresh possibilities emerge that offer leads to progress. Changes in your home and daily life bring a productive and active environment that advances your situation forward. You benefit from staying flexible and innovative; harnessing the power of creativity offers a fast track towards your dreams.

Under a prosperous influence, you discover it's best to release the areas you have outgrown. It moves you to the next level, and moving on cuts the path wide open with fresh possibilities. It does bring a time when your abilities are activated and amplified. You set your goals in motion and capitalize on inspiring energy that ramps up the success possible.

Your priorities are shifting, which can take you away from certain people in your more full social circle. As you drift away from these characters, you draw new potential into your world. It brings those who inspire your heart and encourage you to move forward in alignment with a soul journey. A key component of success is investigating new leads.

It helps you create a shift that offers you substantial rewards. As you set your sights on developing your vision, you can embark on a bold chapter that propels you towards a journey of expansive optimism. It brings a fresh perspective; you broaden your perception and release any doubt that holds you back. Shifting to an abundant mindset draws rewards. It does let you replenish and restock your reserves.

A downshift draws emotional awareness; it puts a more profound layer into your life. If you trust yourself to make the right decisions, it becomes the catalyst that enables you to create your abundance. You touch down on a scene that inspires and reinvigorates your personal life. It does bring new adventures and lively outings into your world. As you make headway on developing a particular goal, you embrace bonding sessions with this person. It does bring change and growth, and this lets you build your life in a more efficient, rewarding manner. It does see you pouring your energy into a journey that is enriching.

A New Moon in Virgo combines with Mercury retrograde ending this week. It does bring foundations that help you join forces with others; with everything changing so quickly, thinking about structure and planning for the future is beneficial. It is a time for new ideas and information; it does bring valuable resources that have you exploring new possibilities. You sharpen your mind and get creative with innovative thinking. It does bring essential changes that open a path forward. It does see power and strength arrive to deliver a boost. If you have found your energy flagging recently, this brings inspiration, which leads to a productive environment. It focuses on long-term plans, and a fruitful mission crops up that inspires your mind. If things feel overwhelming at this time, you can appreciate the changes ahead. It does bring clues of new opportunities that surface to expand your life towards an original path. It does heighten the potential possible and marks a significant turning point.

Good news ahead brings a significant shift forward that teams you up with rising prospects. It offers an uptick of new options that have you feeling energized and ready to tackle new projects with a view towards advancement. You discover a unique opportunity that captures the essence of inspiration and enables you to build grounded foundations that offer room to improve home life. A new role on offer brings inspiration and heightened security.

Mabon/Fall Equinox occurs this week with a Full Moon, Supermoon in Aries towards the week's end. You wipe the slate clean and release outworn areas. This lunar healing yields the highest sense of stability that renews and rejuvenates your life. You refuel energy tanks and push back the barriers that have limited progress. It does draw research that opens a new direction. It places you in a solid position to move forward and learn a new area. Expanding your life nourishes well-being and draws equilibrium into your surroundings. You are on a journey of growth and evolution. Staying flexible and adaptable helps you skip over any bumps in the road without becoming derailed. Increased stability brings a grounded and secure foundation to grow your vision.

News arrives that becomes a windfall; the shining star guides your path forward. It does see life becoming busy and brings an active and productive environment that offers a sense of progression and growth. You enjoy the bustling phase of potential that tempts you forward. Lively social interaction draws well-being.

Removing areas that are no longer in alignment with your vision does create space for the new potential to flow into your world. You are currently on a journey that brings possibilities to light that advance your goals. It focuses on your dreams and developing a progressive and prosperous path. News arrives to point the way forward.

Sun	Mon	Tue	Wed	Thu	Fri	Sat
1	2	3	4	5	6	7
8	9	10	11	12	13	14
15	16	17	18	19	20	21
22	23	24	25	26	27	28
29	30	31				

October 6th - Last Quarter Moon in Cancer 13.48

October 7th - Draconids Meteor Shower. Oct 6th-10th

October 11th - Pluto Retrograde ends in Capricorn

October 14th - New Moon in Libra 17:54
October 14th - Annular Solar Eclipse 17:59

October 20th - Mercury at Superior Conjunction

October 21st -Orionids Meteor Shower. Oct 2nd – Nov 7th

October 22nd - First Quarter Moon Aquarius 03.29

October 23rd - Venus at Greatest Elong: 46.4°W

October 28th - Partial Lunar Eclipse 20:14
October 28th - Hunters Full Moon in Taurus 20:23

NEW MOON

FULL MOON

Mercury heads to your second house of possessions, acquisitions, substance, and material wealth. It is ideal for contemplating the path ahead using research and strategy. You can get creative and concentrate on areas that speak to your heart. It does encourage you to brush up on your skills and explore new options. You obtain maximum results with a willingness to ferret out opportunities that may not be obvious at first. Information arrives that draws a wellspring of potential into your world. Trailblazing conversations nurture growth and bring essence to ideas. Developing concrete plans helps achieve success. Nourishing and cultivating your goals offer particular value that promotes advancement during this time. It does let you open a gateway towards growth. Being receptive to change enables you to make the most of an enterprising chapter ahead. It does set sail to a new adventure that offers you room to grow your situation. You stake your claim on a journey that brings inspiration, and it has you excited to be planning for future growth. You release all that stands in your way between you and success.

It does see new potential flowing into your world that is a breath of fresh air. It lifts the cloud that you may have felt under recently. Options to improve your home environment align you with a social chapter that is a wellspring of potential. It does give you the chance to chart your course towards a personal goal. Being open and flexible is key to expanding your options.

Pluto retrograde ends in Capricorn. New Moon in Libra at the week's end combines with an annular solar eclipse. Pluto turning direct brings power and transformation into your life. It offers the depth, intensity, and metamorphosis that cultivates change. Support comes in the form of words of wisdom and guidance. A project you share with your friends draws a golden influx of new possibilities into your life. A compelling Avenue opens, and this brings a curious sideline for you to channel your excess energy into promoting. It does keep your potential soaring high as you move forward towards developing a dream. News arrives, which brings a boost to your life.

You reach a crossroads that draws new options. You clear away indecisiveness and take a challenging new role on board. Your skills draw a path that lets you create a powerful transition forward. It enables you to make strides towards growing your abilities. It sees progression take center stage; it pares you up with an opportunity that has you headed in the direction of growth. It gives you space to flex your muscles and dive into a productive chapter.

Significant changes are coming. As you move away from struggle and frustration, limiting beliefs are released, drawing abundance. It does restore equilibrium, giving you a more stable foundation to nurture your vision. A transformation ahead illustrates possibilities that activate creativity. It teams you with an area that offers you room to grow your dreams. It lets you venture further and explore options that tempt you forward.

Mercury at Superior conjunction brings insights from the past to your life. The past has a strong effect on your current energy. It does get a time of resolving outworn power, and this gives you the shift forward that turns out to be quite a blessing. News arrives that improves your situation. It offers a chapter of harmony that draws happiness into your surroundings. Life soon contrasts with events that shake up your environment. It does get a path that takes you towards expansion. You are no stranger to barriers, and while things can feel like an uphill battle, there is the promise of new options that tempt you forward. You show the initiative and make waves. Forging ahead towards your vision and clearing away the cobwebs brings a project you can embrace.

Things are turning full-circle. Staying true to your vision draws a path that, soon enough, leaves you feeling excited and inspired about the possibilities. As your situation flows forward, you move towards developing your idea. It brings a portal, a new chapter; this transitions you to an environment that is ripe with potential. There are indications that confidential information comes to light that brings a happy realization. The past has been a time of coming of age; the learning of wisdom has planted seeds you now can harvest. A venture ahead gives you an environment ripe for progression.

This week, a partial lunar eclipse blends magic with a Full Moon in Taurus. It does bring a time of self-discovery that charts a successful course towards an empowering chapter where you dig deep and cut away outworn areas. It sees a path opening that inspires your mind and encourages a shift towards learning and growth. Sweeping changes occur through your willingness to explore little-worn avenues and think outside the box. Your gifts are ready to be channeled into an inspiring endeavor.

Important news reaches you from a far-flung destination. It does have you feeling fired up about a new path. It speaks of the opportunity to begin a new chapter. This path boosts positive energy, is the perfect elixir for banishing the doldrums, and releasing outworn areas that are no longer relevant. Indeed, creating space to build a new foundation draws dividends. Your life heads towards an uptick of movement and change.

When news arrives, you reach a turning point that bodes well for your circumstances. It does bring a refreshing viewpoint, and this connects you with people and opportunities. A more social environment takes you in a direction that supports your personal growth. A changing scene on the horizon has you feeling inspired about the possibilities. Surprise news lights an exciting path forward. It does blaze a trail towards an active chapter.

Sun	Mon	Tue	Wed	Thu	Fri	Sat
			1	2	3	4
5	6	7	8	9	10	11
12	13	14	15	16	17	18
19	20	21	22	23	24	25
26	27	28	29	30		

November 3rd - Jupiter at Opposition

November 4th - Saturn Retrograde ends in Pisces

November 4th - Taurids Meteor Shower.Sept 7th - Dec 10th

November 5th - Last Quarter Moon in Leo 08:37

November 13th - Uranus at Opposition
November 13th - New Moon in Scorpio 09:27

November 17th - Leonids Meteor Shower Nov 6th -30th

November 18th - Mars in Conjunction with Sun

November 20th - First Quarter Moon in Aquarius 10.50

November 27th – Beaver Moon. Full Moon in Gemini 09:16

FULL MOON

Jupiter at opposition. Saturn retrograde ends in Pisces. Saturn brings a focus on structure, stability, and discipline. It donates a time of hard work that provides fruitful results. You are on a beautiful journey towards improving your circumstances. You soon ground your energy in an area that lets you gain traction on developing an exciting goal. Opportunity comes knocking and brings expansion into your life. Experimenting and exploring options brings the right flavor into your life. It positions you to achieve growth and progress life forward onto new endeavors. You soon receive news about an offer that feels tempting and tailor-made for your life.

New goals and an inspiring vision help raise confidence. Implementing functional changes grows your life in a structured and balanced manner. You can reshuffle the deck and come out with advancement for your career path. It's a time imbued with possibility and potential. It offers to refine and upskill your talents into a new area. A fresh cycle begins that helps you move away from stormy seas and enter calmer waters. It provides a sturdy foundation that improves structure and balance around your home life. It brings plenty of new exploring opportunities that give you the green light to connect with inspiration and creativity. It lets you integrate beneficial changes that bring a grounded foundation into your life.

The planet Uranus is in opposition as the New Moon occurs in Scorpio. You enter a cycle of increasing abundance that offers a radiant aspect. It carries news and information worth celebrating; it sweeps in the kind of potential that jumpstarts growth in your social circle. It marks a time of communication that lights the path forward to a more connected environment. Life fills with magic and excitement as your social life becomes active and dynamic. It triggers opportunities to mingle and connect with friends.

A change of scene on the horizon is therapeutic and beneficial for your spirit. It draws an enterprising time that shines a floodlight on developing your personal life. Nurturing your dreams and building stable foundations improves harmony and brings blessings into your world. It delivers an essential time of sharing thoughts and ideas with someone who cultivates happiness in your life. Advancement ahead provides the chance to develop a meaningful journey forward for your romantic life.

A bonanza of new possibilities raises the potential in your life. It brings a perk that has you pleased about the progress possible. It brings luck and good fortune to walk by your side as you expand horizons into new areas. Impending improvement draws blessings. An opportunity comes up that sees your creativity rising. It brings the good news that can deliver tangible results.

Leonids Meteor Shower. Mars in conjunction with the Sun. Changes ahead bring inspiration flowing into your life. The influence from Mars this week ignites a journey of passion and adventure. It lets you step into the spotlight and embrace a social aspect that connects you with friends and colleagues. It illuminates a chance for collaboration as lively discussions get the ball rolling on exploring ideas for ventures and projects. It lets you team up with an environment that offers rising prospects. A focus on building your dreams draws a pleasing result. Immersing yourself in an exciting area gives purpose and substance to your world. It helps set up a long-term structure around your home life. It brings goals to work towards, and many possibilities flow into your world; each represents something new on offer. It brings a time of personal growth that enriches your life.

You breeze through an ample time of expanding opportunities. Your rising creativity sparkles brightly, driving confidence. It brings a path packed with happy surprises and new possibilities. Your mission to improve your circumstances helps you make substantial gains around stability as you nurture ideas suitable for progression. It brings a sterling opportunity that shares your talents with a broader audience. Every detail counts as you expand your world into new areas. It gets a busy time ahead.

The Full Moon in Gemini supports your growth and evolution. News arrives that is a windfall. An area you focus on does move forward. It helps you take advantage of a fresh flow of energy that breaks up outworn areas. The fires of inspiration burning brightly in your life. It does let you sail to smoother waters. This Full Moon brings a sense of relief; it allows you to feel that you are making progress in life where it is most needed.

Indeed, it does show that heightened stability is the outcome of being involved with shedding outworn layers. As you peel back areas that are no longer relevant, you break fresh ground and create space for the new potential to blossom. It lets you see the path ahead more clearly. You find your feet after what has been a destabilizing chapter.

It is time that sees you becoming quite busy. Events play out in your favor when you can grow your world. An offer lands at your feet. It does add up to a productive and lively environment. You see changes around your life that offer a sense of progression and growth.

All in all, this improves the stability of the home front. It does give you more options and places you in the box seat to expand your life into a new area. You enter a happy chapter that brings innovative changes. There are adjustments made that define the path and create a smoother environment.

DECEMBER

Sun	Mon	Tue	Wed	Thu	Fri	Sat
					1	2
3	4	5	6	7	8	9
10	11	12	13	14	15	16
17	18	19	20	21	22	23
24	25	26	27	28	29	30
31						

December 4th - Mercury at Greatest Elong: 21.3°E

December 5th - Last Quarter Moon in Virgo 05:49

December 6th - Neptune Retrograde ends in Pisces

December 12th - New Moon in Sagittarius 23:32

December 13th - Geminids Meteor Shower. Dec 7th - 17th
December 13th - Mercury Retrograde begins in Capricorn

December 19th - First Quarter Moon Pisces 18:39

December 21st - Ursids Meteor Shower Dec 17th -25th

December 22nd - Yule/Winter Solstice at 03:28
December 22nd - Mercury at Inferior Conjunction

December 27th - Cold Moon. Moon Before Yule. Full Moon in Cancer 00:34

December 31st - Jupiter Retrograde ends in Taurus

FULL MOON

Neptune retrograde ends in Pisces, bringing a dreamy aspect that can cloud your vision if you don't create plans to match your goals. This week is an ideal time to start thinking about the path ahead and jot down some plans for the future. It heightens creativity and offers structure and stability as it takes your talents to the next level. A positive change ahead brings a new vista that develops your skills. It brings advancement into your life.

Allow things to unfold, and know you can handle all that comes your way over the coming weeks. A busy time brings the essence of wanderlust into your life. It starts an exciting journey that grows your world outwardly. It does get time to work with your abilities as you nurture the potential possible in your life. Rising prospects draw a path glittering with golden options. It offers advancement, which lets you achieve the best results possible.

Finding the right path is essential in cracking the code to achieve your vision. Being adaptable, flexible, and going after creative solutions help unearth the right way ahead for your life. Setting goals sets an important intention that empowers you to move forward with courage and conviction to develop your life journey. You turn a corner soon, bringing more stability into your life. Secret information opens the path ahead. It does draw new possibilities to your social life that connects you with a kindred spirit.

The New Moon is in Sagittarius this week, with Mercury going retrograde the day afterward. Weeding out areas that limit progress streamlines the path ahead. It helps you work efficiently and effectively to achieve a higher level of growth. The excellent you resonate mirrors back into your life in the form of new opportunities. It brings a direction that has you feeling enthusiastic about the potential possible. Focusing on your vision enables you to soar beyond everyday limitations and forge ahead towards your goals. It leads to dabbling in a new interest that is thought-provoking and inspiring.

It is of a time of messages that reveal secret information. News arrives that gives you insight into your broader community environment. It helps to solve outworn areas, and it gives you insight into someone who has been disingenuous with you. This person puts on a fake front and runs tales to others. You soon realize that this person has a chameleon-like ability.

Open communication lights the way forward. Your attention switches to your private life and the care and attention to detail draw a pleasing result. Good luck and harmony flow into your personal life, enabling outworn energy to dissolve. If problems recur, noticing the potential issues around the Mercury retrograde phase allows you to pivot away from obstacles and blend your path towards a higher result. An experimental flavor lets you make changes intuitively to draw comfort and security.

Ursids Meteor Shower promotes bright blessings in your life. A new option ahead connects you with a social environment. It brings a productive time that bids farewell to setbacks and hurdles. It draws liberation, freedom, and expansion. Your willingness to push back barriers plays an integral part in revealing possibilities that tempt you forward.

Life picks up speed and becomes more active as you turn the corner and head towards a dynamic environment. It gives you a chance to rebrand your life and reinvent yourself in a new area. It expands your social circle with new companions. A surge of optimism lets you explore the potential for your personal life. It draws a social aspect that brings a lovely and supportive environment into view. It marks a chance to expand horizons as an offer to mingle is coming up. Social engagement beckons, and it opens your life to new characters. It is a time of change with plenty to keep you feeling inspired.

Life takes a busy turn which draws an active environment. You may find yourself dealing with many demands at once; multitasking, juggling, and delegating will help you adjust to the productive pace. It brings a vibrant atmosphere that keeps optimism humming along. It lights a path of inspiration that supports growth and expansion. It translates to a time that lets you focus on enjoying life to the fullest. Cheered on by friends and colleagues, you feel the wind beneath your wings.

Yule/Winter Solstice at the beginning of the week with a Full Moon in Cancer midweek, followed by Jupiter retrograde ending on the last day of the year in Taurus. It is a delicate time that lets you look within and see the needed changes to strip away outworn areas. It brings a low-key environment that enables you to explore future options focusing on planning. Exploring new avenues opens a path that delivers a simple solution. It is a previously unseen way, and this avenue improves your circumstances. It is the shift towards a harmonious phase of growth.

You can bet that life holds an exciting change. It does take you on a journey of new horizons. It speaks of movement and discovery; you can grow and expand your life. It seems that new things are afoot, which takes you towards a happy chapter. A willingness to be open to new possibilities helps draw this positive energy into your life.

The seeds planted during this time ripen and blossom over the coming chapter. It does bring opportunities for you to be involved in a more social environment. It highlights developing long-held goals and dreams. You draw new friendships to light as you test the waters in fresh territory. It does bring a sense of connection and abundance to the forefront of your life. This week is an extraordinary time that grows your strength. It draws changes you can appreciate in time.

NOTES

Astrology, Tarot & Horoscope Books.

https://mystic-cat.com/

Printed in Great Britain
by Amazon

13072214R00071